# The Engineer & the Vaccine

## By Steven Raimondi

Steven's Steam Books
San Jose, California

S

**Special Thanks**

I would like to extend my heartfelt thanks and admiration to my very patient and talented editor, Laura Duggan, my illustrator, Laurie Hartsook, and my book designer, Connie King. They have been the most positive and encouraging folks I could imagine working with. They were always so helpful and patient in explaining details about becoming a self-published author. I look forward to working with them again.

Copyright © 2021 by Steven Raimondi

All rights reserved. No part of this book may be reproduced or transmitted in any form or by any means, electronic or mechanical, including photocopying, recording, or by any information storage and retrieval system, or internet program or system, without written permission from the author.

Editor: Laura Duggan
Illustrator: Laurie Hartsook
Book design & publishing services:
Constance King Design

Steven's Steam Books
San Jose, California
www.stevensteambooks.com

Printed in USA
ISBN: 978-1-7379911-0-6

One quiet spring night, an eight-year-old boy named Jimmy was going to bed. After he got under the blankets, his mother, Caitlin, came up to him and said, "Sweetheart, Grandma and Grandpa will be here in the morning to take you for your sleep over."

"I'm excited for that, Mom," Jimmy answered with a smile. His Grandma Fiona and Grandpa Thomas were gentle, kind-hearted people. Thomas used to be an engineer, a person that drove trains on the railroad, and Jimmy loved hearing about Grandpa's exciting adventures on the rails. "I love staying with Grandma and Grandpa," he added.

"I know you do," Caitlin answered. Then she added, "Before they take you to your sleep over, you have to go to the doctors for your vaccination shot."

With a frightened look on his face, Jimmy said, "No! Mom I don't want to. Yesterday, one of my friends next door came home from the doctor's office and she was crying. She told me she got a vaccination shot and it hurt."

Caitlin was surprised at what Jimmy said.

"Jimmy, it's not as bad as you think. I got my vaccination last week, and it was just a little pinch that lasted just a second," she said, trying to ease her son's worry."

Jimmy replied,

# "Mom, I don't like getting pinched."

"Nobody really does, but it's not that bad, and it's to help keep us healthy," she said, rubbing her son's head.

He looked like he was about to argue some more when his mother said, "Jimmy, let's not talk about it anymore tonight. Think about the fun you will have at your sleepover," she gave her son a kiss goodnight and said, "I'll see you in the morning."

Not long after Caitlin left her son's room, she went to the phone and made a call to her father. "Dad, do you think you and Mom could come early tomorrow?" she asked.

Thomas was surprised at this. "How come?" he asked his daughter.

Caitlin said, "Jimmy has to get his vaccine tomorrow, but he doesn't want to go to the doctor. He's afraid."

Thomas replied, "Don't worry, we'll be there after breakfast."

The next morning at nine o'clock, Jimmy was finishing his breakfast. Just then, there was a knock at the door, and his mother left the kitchen. After Jimmy finished his breakfast, he went into the living room, where he was surprised to see his grandparents. His face lit up with a smile, as he ran up to them crying, "Grandma. Grandpa." He then gave them a big hug.

After that they settled down on the sofa, and Thomas said to his grandson, "Your mother called us last night and told us you're afraid to get a vaccination shot."

"Yes," Jimmy answered, looking down with a sad look.

Thomas put his arm around Jimmy and said,

# "Jimmy, vaccination shots are nothing to be afraid of."

"Back when I was driving trains on the Santa Fe, our whole town was as scared as you're feeling now."

Fiona added, "Our town changed its feelings when your grandfather took a chance to get vaccine to help everyone. He was a hero after that."

Jimmy was surprised to hear that. He then asked, "Is that true?"

"It is," Thomas answered with a smile. "It all happened just before your grandmother and I got married.

"Can you tell me the story, Grandpa?" Jimmy asked.

"Of course, I can," Thomas answered.

"I think you'll be surprised to hear how I managed to show everyone that vaccines are good for people."

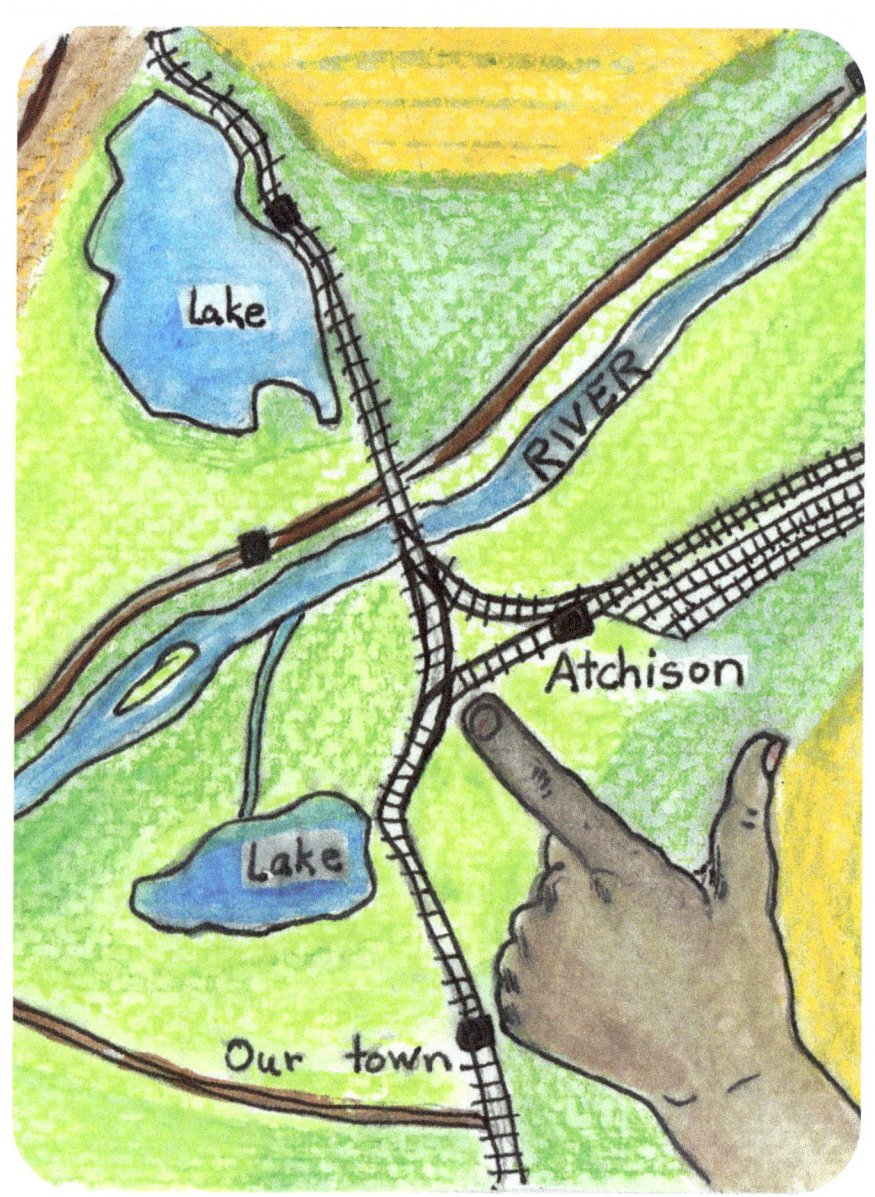

This
was the story
Thomas
told Jimmy.

Years ago, Thomas was an engineer on the Atchison, Topeka, and Santa Fe Railroad, or the Santa Fe for short. Thomas drove a handsome engine that had a blue boiler, accented with a red cowcatcher, headlight, wheels, and domes. Other features had included a brown cab and a

green tender, and a straight smokestack with a diamond design at the top. Thomas loved being an engineer for the railroad, driving Santa Fe engine number seven, and he always looked forward to seeing Fiona at the end of each of his runs.

One day, in the middle of summer that year, a disease called small pox was making some townsfolk sick. Thomas, like many, hoped that it wouldn't reach their town. Things seemed to be alright, until one day a strange man came to town. The man got off the stage coach, he was feeling hot, and he was feeling like he was going to faint.

He entered the hotel and asked for a room to stay in. "Could I have some cool water, please?" he asked.

The hotel manager said happily, "Certainly sir. Why don't you sign the register while I get you some water?"

Not long after the man signed the register, he fell down. The manager raced up to the man. Helping the stranger to the sofa, he noticed the sheriff's deputy passing by the front door and called to him, "Get the doctor! This man needs help."

The deputy raced toward the doctor's office, and soon after a crowd started to gather outside the hotel. The sheriff arrived to keep the crowd back. Walking down the street, Thomas and Fiona saw the crowd. "What's going on Thomas?" she asked worriedly.

"I don't know Fiona," Thomas answered. He then saw the town doctor, Doctor Carter, heading toward the hotel and said, "Looks like someone is sick or injured."

Curious, they went over and stood back from the crowd, and watched Doctor Carter enter the hotel. Inside, the doctor asked the hotel manager, "So, what happened? Tell me about it."

The manager answered, "He said he felt dizzy and hot, and felt sick to his stomach. He's kept his eyes closed these past few minutes."

Doctor Carter was surprised to notice a rash on the man's skin. He looked serious and asked, "Has anyone else touched him?"

"No, only me," The manager replied. "Why?"

"I'm afraid this man has smallpox," Doctor Carter said gently. Word traveled through the crowd outside making them start to feel scared. Doctor Carter asked the sheriff to keep the people calm while he made an announcement. The sheriff did so, and Doctor Carter said to the people, "Folks, recently there has been a vaccine discovered that cures smallpox, and prevents us from getting it. Towns everywhere have been vaccinating people so they can be safe."

The people looked surprised at the news and started talking among themselves. The sheriff placed the hotel under quarantine and asked the people in the hotel to stay inside. As for the people outside, they had to stay away from the hotel until further notice.

The people were about to walk away and carry on with what it was they were doing when a man named Mr. Morgan spoke up. "Nobody is going to put something like what the doctor just described in me! I think we should all go home and stay away from each other, especially the hotel. In time, this thing will go away."

Thomas didn't like what Mr. Morgan had said. "I think he's wrong," he said to Fiona as the sheriff went by.

"You think we should get vaccinated, Thomas?" Fiona asked.

"Yes," Thomas answered. "We can't stay away from each other forever. Even if we don't get sick now, another visitor could bring it here again."

"I think I see what you're saying," Fiona replied.

The sheriff heard the two. He approached them and

said, "I agree with you both. To be safe we'll all have to be vaccinated. Also, if we don't get the sick man medicine, he won't last long, and we'll risk losing the other people in the hotel."

"I have a plan for how to get the vaccine to the town, and I'll even get vaccinated before I return. I'm sure my fireman Kevin wouldn't mind either," Thomas said with a smile.

"I think that's very kind and brave of you, Thomas," Fiona replied with happiness.

"Let's head on over to the station so I can show you what I had in mind," Thomas said.

As they headed toward the station, what they didn't know was that the townspeople had heard everything. Mr. Morgan piped up and said, "Count me out, I'm going home."

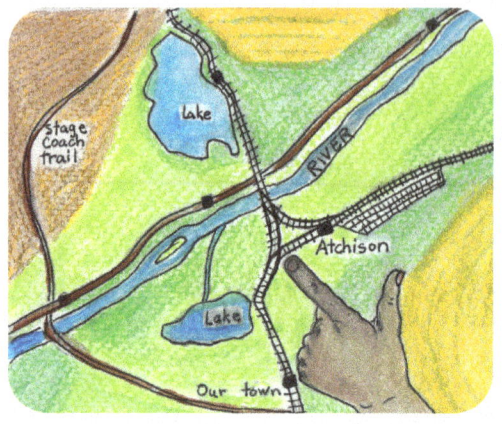

Mr. Morgan walked off, then his wife said to the people, "Don't worry, he'll change his mind."

At the station, Thomas was showing Fiona, the sheriff, and Clint, the station's telegraph operator, the map of the railroad. He pointed to a y-track section not far from the trainyards of Atchison. A y-track was often used for trains to turn around.

"If my engine arrives at this y-track just outside the trainyards at Atchison, it will keep the town and the people there safe. If we sent them a message explaining the situation, maybe they'll bring a doctor from the hospital to meet us with the vaccine," Thomas explained. "Atchison is the closest town to ours, and it's got a hospital that has the vaccine."

"That could work," Clint said in agreement. "We'd better get you permission from the train yard manager to go ahead with the plan."

Clint started tapping the message on the telegraph, and the message was soon being received in the telegraph office at Atchison station. A few minutes later, the telegraph began clicking out the response from Atchison. Clint listened to the telegraph's coded message clicking on the receiver, and began to write it down. As he wrote the message, Thomas, Fiona, and the sheriff looked concerned. However, their faces lit up with smiles as Clint read, "The town of Atchison likes your plan, Thomas. They're going to have one of

their doctors waiting at the y-track with a shipment of vaccine for our town. They think it's brave of you to take the vaccine when you arrive in Atchison."

"Thomas, this is great," Fiona said excitedly.

Just then, Kevin, the fireman for the train, came into the station and asked what was going on. Thomas explained everything. "Thomas," Kevin said with a smile. "I'll get our engine fired up in no time at all."

An hour later in the engine house, engine number seven was steaming nicely. After Thomas brought the engine to the station, he climbed down, and Fiona gave him a hug to wish him luck on the trip. Just as Thomas was about to climb back into the cab, there was someone calling, "Wait."

Thomas turned and said, "Mr. Morgan!" with surprise.

"What brings you here?" Kevin asked.

Mr. Morgan then said gently, "My wife said I was a coward to say what I said to everyone. She said she wouldn't stay away from other people forever, and I would get lonely all by myself at home. I'd like to go with you so I can help you. I don't want my wife to think badly of me. Will you take me with you?"

Thomas smiled and said, "Fiona and I are getting married in two months, so I can understand how you feel. I would never want to disappoint my loved ones, Climb aboard."

"Thank you," Mr. Morgan replied. He climbed into the engine's cab, and Thomas followed him.

"Be safe, Thomas," Fiona said.

"We will," Thomas answered.

Soon they were racing along the rails toward Atchison. The trip was going fast, fortunately, since the dispatcher of the railroad gave them clearance to collect the vaccine and to head directly back, keeping the track clear. Everything was going smoothly. Before long, they spotted another engine and some men up ahead. They arrived in record time. Thomas stopped his engine and backed it onto the y-track so they could head home quickly after they picked up the vaccine.

The three men climbed down from the engine cab and walked to the front of the engine. A doctor named Doctor Lawrence came up to them with another engineer carrying a bowl of hot water.

Doctor Lawrence said, "I heard about you three wanting to be vaccinated right away. I'll do it gladly after I wash my hands with the hot water. Following this, I'll head back with you to vaccinate the people who aren't in the hotel."

"Thank you, Doctor," Thomas replied. He then asked, "I'd like to be vaccinated first if that's alright?"

Doctor Lawrence said, "Of course, that's alright with me." Mr. Morgan and Kevin also agreed. After washing

his hands, Doctor Lawrence got an injection of vaccine ready. Thomas then rolled up his left sleeve, turned his face away, gave Kevin's hand a squeeze and closed his eyes as he was injected with the vaccine. After the injection, he said with a smile, "I've always been nervous around needles since I was pricked with one of my mother's sewing needles. But this wasn't too bad."

"You did great, Thomas," Kevin added, supporting his friend.

Then Mr. Morgan said, "There's no shame in being nervous about some things."

"No argument there," Doctor Lawrence said in agreement. "Some of the people in town, both young and old, feel the same way you do." Thomas smiled hearing this.

Once the three men were vaccinated, they headed back toward home, with Doctor Lawrence and enough vaccine for everyone on board.

At the station, Fiona was waiting on the platform for the train engine. Then she heard the engine's whistle, and soon coming into the station with its bell ringing was Thomas' engine. Thomas waved to Fiona as they arrived, and the people in town came up to the station.

After stopping the train, they unloaded the vaccine, Kevin got some hot water from the engine so Doctor Lawrence could wash his hands, and everyone received the vaccine.

Then everyone headed to the hotel. "Doc," called the sheriff as he knocked on the door.

Doctor Carter opened the door and Thomas said, "We got the vaccine for the people. Everyone in town has been vaccinated."

"Good," Doctor Carter replied with a smile.

Thomas placed the box of vaccine on the walkway and backed away. Then Doctor Carter took the vaccine inside. After waiting a while, Doctor Carter then opened the hotel door and said, "Everyone in the hotel has been vaccinated, including me. The man who had smallpox is feeling much better."

"Excellent," the sheriff said with a smile. "You'll have to keep everyone in there for two weeks so it can take effect."

The Town Council was so grateful for the bravery Thomas exemplified, they created a plaque in his honor and hung it at the entrance of the hotel as a reminder that everyone has the potential to be a hero.

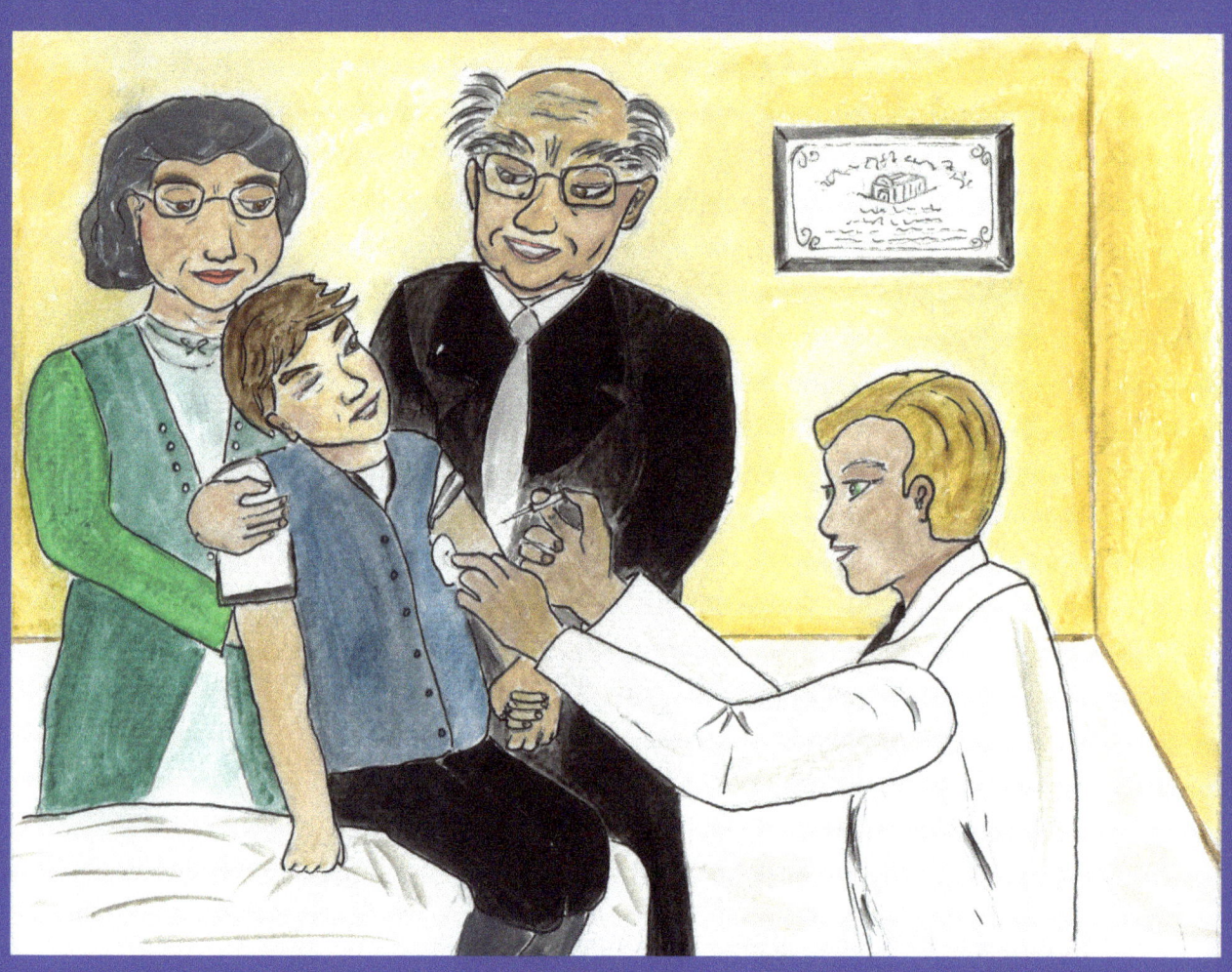

As Thomas finished the story, he said to Jimmy, "After the two weeks had passed, everyone in the hotel was free to see everyone again."

## "Your grandfather was given a hero's praise for his courage in showing how important it was to receive vaccines," Fiona added.

"Wow," Jimmy said amazed. "Grandpa, I didn't know."

"Now you do, my boy," Thomas said as he hugged his grandson. He then suggested, "Why don't we go with you? If you need to give my hand a squeeze, you can."

"Okay," Jimmy answered with a smile.

When they arrived at the doctor's office, Jimmy looked toward his grandfather with his eyes closed and squeezed his hand while the doctor injected him with vaccine. After that the doctor placed a bandage over where the injection given.

## "You did a good job, Jimmy," the doctor said with a smile.

"Thanks doctor," Jimmy answered. "Grandpa helped me earlier when he told me his story about vaccines." The doctor smiled at the news.

The next day Jimmy and Thomas went to the local train museum, and on display was Thomas' engine number seven. Jimmy was glad his grandfather told him the story about the importance of getting vaccinated.

Jimmy learned that it was alright to be afraid,
but with help from people we love we can do anything.

Jimmy, and his family knew that vaccines save lives.

# Message from the Author

I know how it feels to be afraid of things. I am afraid of needles, including vaccination needles. I've never been fond of getting vaccination shots because I was always worried getting it would hurt. At the same time, I know that they are important for my health, so I always have a relative with me so we can hold hands. I close my eyes and keep them covered so I don't see what is happening. I did that when I had my vaccination for Covid-19. There is no shame in being afraid of getting vaccinated. If you are afraid, I suggest doing what I do, and it will help you get through your vaccination shot. Having a friend or a loved one nearby can help you get through scary situations.

# About the Author

Howdy, folks! My name is Steven Raimondi. Call me Steven. Ever since I was a little boy, I've been obsessed with steam trains. It all started when I was about two years old and I fell in love with my grandfather's old Lionel steam train engine # 233, Smokey by name. As I watched Smokey work his magic by racing along those little tracks and watched his rods moving, I fell in love with steam trains.

Today, my passions include steam trains, steam ships, classic cars, and classic films (especially Disney). As an old-fashioned, autistic adult, I live with my family in San Jose, California. I was never a fan of writing in school but always loved daydreaming. I have found writing to be a wonderful way to share my ideas with others.

For further information about the author and other books he has written, visit his website at: www.stevensteambooks.com

CPSIA information can be obtained
at www.ICGtesting.com
Printed in the USA
BVHW020730080222
628274BV00019B/170